"*Walking and Wayfinding* cannot help but make you walk. Which is a good thing. As Lea Appleton so invitingly lays out, walking mindfully can be a contemplative practice. This book is a star in the night sky of our lives' sea journey. It orients us; and helps us find our way."

—Frank Rogers Jr., professor of spiritual formation at the Claremont School of Theology and author of *Cradled in the Arms of Compassion*.

"So often spiritual practices seem out of reach, both in the time they require and in the particular skills they demand. But then along comes Lea Appleton, suggesting another possibility, beckoning us to join her in just a little stroll. And the very simplicity of the form (even if it may exhaust us at times—as all journeys can) opens us to the Universe of Truth and Beauty that flows in and through and around every moment of our winding pilgrimage through this world."

—Andrew Dreitcer, Vice President for Academics and Dean of the Faculty at Claremont School of Theology.

WALKING &
WAYFINDING

WALKING & WAYFINDING

Create Your Own Mindful Practice,
One Step at a Time

LEA APPLETON

Roadmap Press

This is a Wayfinding Series Book
Published by Roadmap Press
Copyright © 2024 by Lea Appleton

www.appletoncoaching.com/roadmap
Appleton, Lea, author
Walking & Wayfinding: Create your own mindful practice, one step at a time
Claremont, California: Roadmap Press, 2024

Library of Congress Control Number: 2024905349
ISBN: 979-8-9901134-0-4 (print)
ISBN: 979-8-9901134-1-1 (e-book)

BODY, MIND & SPIRIT / Mindfulness
SELF-HELP / Journaling / Personal Growth
SPORTS & RECREATION / Walking

Cover design by Carolyn Knapp
Author photograph by Michael Negrete
Photographs courtesy of Lea Appleton

DEDICATION

For Billy,

the one with whom I walk

until the end of time

CONTENTS

PREFACE

My walking practice started in earnest as a response to missing out on an opportunity to walk. For over a year I had been preparing to walk the Camino de Santiago in Spain with my sister in May 2020. It's a series of pilgrimage routes that takes many days, even weeks to complete on foot, depending on which path you choose. But a worldwide pandemic hampered those plans and the trip got cancelled. Initially, I had been understanding that this probably was a good enough reason for my experience to be called off, but as the months went on, my disappointment increased. Because time and money resources were less abundant for me a couple of years later (as I was launching my coaching practice) and it wasn't feasible for me to plan an international trip as the world began opening up again, I decided to create my own pilgrimage. It was a DIY response to work with what I had available to me at the time. Thus, in February 2022, I walked over 70 miles along the coast of Southern California from my home to my sister's home. Over the course of five days, I walked and stayed in small beach hotels along the way.

I discovered several things on this pedestrian journey. I discovered how much I loved being outside. I discovered how long it takes me to quiet my head when I walk. I discovered how eating when (really) hungry and sleeping when (really) tired are especially delicious. I discovered that I wanted to keep doing this kind of walking even more. I took up a regular walking practice in the hopes of creating an annual DIY Pilgrimage.

The following year, I found my time and financial resources even more limited. Yet these restrictions allowed me to create a day-long walk that I named a Wayfinding Day. I walked nearly 20 miles along a different stretch of coastline on a Sunday in February. My Wayfinding Day was more possible for me as it didn't involve hotel stays and multiple days away from work.

I walked with the intention to notice and reflect and journal my way through the day. I did some of that and I mostly walked in quiet. What I learned as I walked was that it still took me a long time to quiet my thoughts!

And the intentions for my journey this time changed over the course of the day. I thought I was walking to figure some things out for myself. I intended to carry a question and come up with an answer, a solution. But instead of a solution, I found peace.

I realized that at least on that day, with the sounds of ocean waves crashing, and bicycle bells ringing, and lots of chatter going on around me, that I turned inward beyond the question that my mind was trying to solve. And I discovered that I didn't need to answer that question after all. Maybe it was getting into a rhythm of my steps or breathing or maybe it was simple fatigue, but my mind joined the rest of my body and was content to hang out. When I was finished for the day, I felt more refreshed and renewed than tired.

I was excited to know that I didn't need five days of walking or an overseas adventure to get a taste of some mindful walking. I was onto something, though not sure what at the time. I wanted to do this again, so this experience renewed my commitment to my regular walking practice, extending some of my daily walks even further.

As I shared the walking experiences that I had created for myself with other people, many responded that they wanted to do something like these mindful and intentional walking moments, too. So, I designed and shared three additional Wayfinding Days for small groups of friends, family, and acquaintances along different parts of the coastline, covering a total of about 50 miles throughout that summer. It wasn't the mileage that was significant, but rather the reflections that took place along those miles of coastal beauty. Through these first small group Wayfinding Days I experimented with different lengths and time frames and discovered that walking for wayfinding didn't even have to happen over the course of one very long day.

I continued my regular walking practice and I began to imagine how more people in even more places could go wayfinding— more than I alone could guide along the coastline in my home state. And I took my wayfinding even closer to home and began to do it as I walked around the block. So can you. And the idea for this book was born.

Lea Appleton
Claremont, CA
November 2023

FOREWORD

Imagine you are chatting comfortably with a trusted friend. The two of you listen deeply and with care to the words of the other. Laughter and delight fill the air between you as your thoughtful conversation generates new ideas and newer possibilities for your health and well-being.

Your imagined precious gift of time is like this book. And Lea, its author, your trusted friend.

Lea has walked the walk, quite literally, that she introduces here as wayfinding. Finding your way—a way that is unique to you, tailored by you for you—from a plethora of possible paths, and despite any number of competing directions. Wayfinding is what Lea practices in her own multi-faceted life— as a scholar, an academic, a musician, administrator, professional certified coach, author, spouse, mother, friend, daughter, sister, hiker, backpacker, camper, and colleague—equipping her as a proficient guide for you in your own varied wayfinding experiences.

As I read this book and considered its many prompts, I was reminded of those large folded paper maps some of our parents carried on family road trips long ago. Like those essential guides from a pre-digital age, you are encouraged to open this treasure in your hands to whatever section first catches your interest. Meander through its outline as you would a lovely scenic road. Notice the landscape it enhances within you. Unfold the chapters of this book, like the sections of that old map, and by following the prompts provided here, you will be taking another few steps on your personal wayfinding path.

This book is consistently interactive and its information exceptionally accessible. Lea offers insights from her own experiences to complement a variety of important prisms in wayfinding, including practice, noticing, awareness, being present and curious, reading the signs and taking a rest. Each chapter provides helpful questions and moments to pause and reflect. You'll want to carry this journal along with you on your wayfinding experiences, whether those experiences take you around the block or around the globe or around the patterns of your own brain.

Lea's guiding presence walks with you, via her instructive words and her thoughtful questions, inviting you to join in her exuberance for finding ways to live the life we are given each day.

Use this book as a guide, a map, a conversation partner, a confidante. And, I guarantee you, you will find your way.

Sharon Rae Graff
Author of *Gratitude Haiku*
(forthcoming Fall 2024, by Elyssar Press)

Lea preparing for the Camino de Santiago in the local wilderness park.

CHAPTER 1
WAYFINDING

If you look at studies in wayfinding, everything from exhibit design to building the cathedrals, it's about creating a complete system. It's about looking at the whole.

—Clement Mok

People walk for many reasons. To get from point A to point B. For fitness or to improve health. To meditate. To be outside and experience nature or the city around them. To explore new surroundings. To get outdoors and away from stress. To walk off anger or anxiousness. To enjoy the weather. To take a break from work. To get to and from work. And people walk to find their way.

Over the course of history, wayfinding is a term in the English language used to talk about navigation, like using the stars to guide a ship in open sea. In contemporary US culture, at least, wayfinding is most often used to describe the process people use to navigate private and public spaces by using signage, as well as for spaces where people can navigate more intuitively by just finding their way. From university and corporate campuses to buildings or municipal outdoor spaces, architects and planners post labels, instructions, directional arrows, etc. and call the process wayfinding.

I'm intrigued by this idea of finding our way, both by using what is in front of us and by sensing the direction we want to go by using other types of cues that we might not even be aware of initially. For me, the process of wayfinding is the act of noticing both internal and external "signage," and making meaning from it. When I walk, I am better able to pay attention to where I am going and maybe you will, too.

I invite you on this path to create for yourself opportunities to notice and become more aware of what is going on inside of you as well as what is going on around you. In doing so I believe that you will experience connection, to yourself and to place. And it is in those points of connection where wayfinding happens and you can feel complete and whole.

You are welcome to read this book in the way you might read other books, from start to finish. You are also invited to explore a chapter that looks interesting to you in whatever order you choose. While the following chapters do build upon one another, anyone who knows me well is aware that I am all for doing things in your own way! So, if you wish to skip around, go to it.

Each chapter starts with a quote for reflection, then a story or some ideas followed by questions for you to answer. I've left space for you to jot some words or draw something in response to the questions, but please create more space in a journal if that is what suits you best. If you choose to record your thoughts and ideas elsewhere, use the space between the questions to reflect a bit about how you might answer if you and I were talking.

There is always a notation for a place to walk marked as [walk here.] This is not so much a command as an invitation, so please use it as such. There are some suggestions for creating a regular walking practice and at the end of the book is a chapter with ideas for how to create your own DIY Wayfinding Day, or extended, reflective walking experience.

This book asks questions that invite you to wonder. You are welcome to journal (write or draw or doodle) before, during or after you walk. The practice is the walking and wondering, and also ultimately, the awareness and insight that comes from doing both. It is the crossroads where intention and attention meet. If you wish to document that crossroads by journaling, please feel free. If you want to hold onto the ideas in other ways, choose the ways that work best for you.

When I walk, I am searching for time and space to be. I want to create an environment where I can live well, thrive, grow, accept, and acknowledge who I am, often in relation to the rest of the world around me. That's a tall order for a walk, but it's all true. Wayfinding as I walk invites me to look at the whole of myself and to see myself in relation to a complete system of all that is around me.

As you begin your walking and wondering in response to the questions on the page, it is my hope that you begin to develop your ability to pay attention, to notice, to enhance your awareness, to build your capacity to wonder as you walk, and to spark the curiosity inside you about what else you might find along the way. And from all this, gain insight.

If you haven't taken a walk yet today, now is the time to do it. Even if you are planning a longer Wayfinding Day, go for a walk now. Get into practice of walking.

[walk here]

Time slows down when we are wayfinding. What do you notice when you are not in a rush or a hurry to get somewhere and slow down to the speed of walking?

What new thought or idea or feeling comes to you as you walk?

What do you look forward to for the rest of your day now that you've taken a walk?

CHAPTER 2
BEGIN TO MOVE

Walking is the perfect way of moving if you want to see into the life of things.

—Elizabeth von Arnim,
The Adventures of Elizabeth in Rügen

When I headed out on my first Wayfinding Day I wrote this: "I've discovered over this past year that my mind is excruciatingly busy and when I sit it spins—seeking resolution, solving problems, searching. But when I move my body, my thoughts slow and I find deep clarity in that inner stillness." There are probably others of you who share that itchy sense of needing to move in order to stop thinking and clear your minds. While I love the idea of sitting in quiet thought or being still as a meditative practice, I have found that walking is really where I experience the life of things.

Wherever we are in life is where we begin when we walk. We come just as we are, in whatever state of mind and body that we are when we take those first steps. It may begin with a furrowed brow trying endlessly to figure something out. Perhaps it's with achy joints or sore muscles. Or maybe it's relief in your heart for some open space.

I try to walk every day, so I have gotten used to walking in whatever shape I am in.

Whether it's a quick trip around the block in between coaching clients or a more leisurely stroll in the evening with my husband. Walking has become part of my regular routine. In fact, it's almost ritual—the act of walking reminds me that I live in a body and not just a mind. Walking connects my mind to and with the rest of my body and it connects me to the world outside of myself. It also gives me opportunity for beauty and delight in my days.

A note about journaling: Sometimes I write as I go because I want to capture the thoughts and ideas that arise as I walk. Other times, I follow the thoughts and what else opens up for me and then journal about them afterwards. In these instances, I often cannot remember the thread of how I got there as I have left those thoughts on my walk. It depends on your intention on whether or not you want to document the process or the outcome of the walk. Or you may just want to walk and see what happens—I often just do that.

[walk here]

What does walking do for you?

What do you find you have more of when you walk?

What do you find you have less of when you walk?

Lea walking by the side of the road (no sidewalk).

CHAPTER 3
SLOW YOUR PACE

*I like walking because it is slow, and I
suspect that the mind, like the feet,
works at about three miles an hour. If this
is so, then modern life is moving faster
than the speed of thought or
thoughtfulness.*

—Rebecca Solnit, *Wanderlust*

While I'd like to say I always was connected to walking, my walking life began after I no longer could run for fitness. My joints have been in the process of giving out for a few decades now. So, initially, I walked out of desperation. I needed to move my body, to get some exercise, and generate some endorphins. I wasn't a completely reluctant walker—I simply wanted to be doing something else.

But what happened over time, especially as I prepared for my Camino experience that didn't materialize, was that the more I walked, the more I discovered and the more I knew about myself. As I kept walking, the more I understood what makes me tick and the less I desired to do that other thing (running) and found that walking was much more than exercise for me. I feel more connected to place when I walk—the sidewalks in my neighborhood, the paths in my local park, the trails in the mountains close to and far away from home. The pace is slower, so I notice more.

I think that the pace of walking is part of what I appreciate about the experience. It requires energy, but not so much that I don't have any left over for other things. I also think it is the movement. I am quite sure that when I walk, I engage my brain in a different way. This has become my why of walking. It is the time when I engage with myself and what is around me. It is the experience of peace that I have both while I walk and afterwards.

In the mini-journal I made for our small group Wayfinding Days, I had a series of questions that we would stop to answer every hour or so. One of them was play on the word "pace." I asked what we would each need to add to our walking pace to allow us to find peace. And the word had to begin with E because PACE + E = PEACE! Some of the words that were shared were "enthusiasm," "energy," "enjoyment," "enlightenment," and "empowered." Often these words are why we walk: to get more energy or to experience more enjoyment or feel empowered.

[walk here]

Using the prompt described above, what do you add to your pace while you walk to create peace? Or in other words, what is your E?

Steps in Los Angeles, where you are reminded to "chase your dreams" as you walk.

CHAPTER 4
EXPLORE YOUR PATH

As you start to walk out on the way,
the way appears.

—Rumi

I am often curious about words. I love seeing
unusual definitions or usages and how that
might change the way I understand a word.

While I was writing about walking, I explored some of the words that we use to talk about walking in English. Here are some of the words I like:

Amble	Saunter
Tramp	Mosey
Trudge	Stroll
March	Stomp
Trek	Romp
Roam	Perambulate
Hike	Tread
Prowl	Wend one's way
Stalk	Hoof it
Skip	Plod
Move	Ramble
Wander	Meander
Stride	Pace

Think about the words we use for walking: amble, saunter, stroll, trek, stomp (my mother used to say that's how I walked through the house as a teenager!). I like to think of skipping as happy walking with a lift in my step; it's whole-body walking. As you read the list, imagine what it would feel like to walk each different way.

As you go for a walk today, pick a few of the ways to move from this list and see how it changes your walk and your experience of walking. Experiment how you move your body as you meander or stride, as you roam or hoof it.

[walk here]

How do you like to walk?

Which of the ways above did you like most?

Which of the ways above do you like least?

Which ones make you uncomfortable?

Which ones make your body feel most at home?

CHAPTER 5
WALKING (OR NOT)

Walking is a spiritual journey and a reflection of living. Each of us must determine which path to take and how far to walk; we must find our own way, what is right for one may not be for another.

—Edie Littlefield Sundby,
The Mission Walker

Sometimes walking is a challenge for any number of reasons. It might be a physical or emotional limitation that keeps us more sedentary. It could be our environment that doesn't have safe enough spaces for us to be outside. It might be our schedule that makes it hard to have a regular walking practice or days to set aside to walk longer.

So, if walking doesn't work for you all the time or most times or ever, think about what else you could do that helps get you connected to your location, the natural world, or your sense of place. Is it sitting in a window or on a porch or deck or balcony? Is it watching some nature reels on social media or travel videos on TV? Is it listening to some ambient nature sounds like ocean waves, leaves crackling, or rain falling?

What else can you do that helps get you connected to yourself? Is it moving each part of your body? Is it taking in a deep, deep breath, holding it briefly, and letting it out?

Settling into the noticing can happen in lots of different ways. I love walking, but I encourage you to find all the ways for you to navigate your wayfinding in the best manner that you can. Many people walk at the pace of a human heartbeat (somewhere in the 60-80 beats per minute, apparently). If your activity isn't walking, check your pulse or put your hand to your chest to feel your heartbeat. Paying attention to your heartbeat can help you focus.

When we walk or immerse ourselves in another type of focusing activity, we give ourselves time to think, to ruminate, to stew, to roll over thoughts in our minds again and again. And then just let them sit there in a tired jumble as we unravel them. On longer walks, I have the time to get past the thinking and move into to just being.

What is another focused activity that you enjoy? Consider other ways you can immerse yourself so that you can let go of thoughts. Is it listening to music? Is it doing a jigsaw puzzle? Is it a more traditional form of meditation? Is it in community with others or by yourself?

[do your activity here]

What is there once you've given yourself enough time to struggle and solve and plan and optimize and you let go of trying to organize your thoughts?

CHAPTER 6
SET YOUR INTENTION

I come out to these solitudes, where the problem of existence is simplified. I see out and around myself…. This is what I go out to seek. It is as if I always met in those places some grand, serene, immortal, infinitely encouraging— though invisible—companion, and walked with him.

—Henry David Thoreau, *Walden*

Often, I have thought that part of what I seek when I walk is something outside myself, like what I consider to be divine presence— maybe that is who Thoreau's "grand, serene, immortal, [and] infinitely encouraging" companion is. It's also possible that for me it might be more philosophical, and I seek connection to the infinity of time and space. Or perhaps it is more mundane, and I seek becoming one with all of my body, since I live only in my head a little too much.

As I walk, I seek out myself, to be my own companion on this pedestrian journey— visible, embodied, human. It's like I'm looking to truly know who I am. It is as if I see into the window of my own soul rather than just seeing "out and around myself."

Whether I walk on a packed granite path with the desert scrub-covered hills around me, or on sidewalk and driveway, or near sand and sea, I walk with similar intention. In all these places, I go mostly to find myself. To seek clarity of my life's direction, meaning, purpose. To find calm in the midst of my overactive brain and bustling daily life. It truly is my solace. It matters less where I walk and more that I simply go walk.

Walking with intention doesn't always mean that I end up where I expect with my thoughts or feelings on a particular day. When I went on my first Wayfinding Day, I fully intended to get some clarity around a question that had been nagging at the edges of my mind. However, that most definitely did not happen! Instead, I had to let go of that intention and just be in the moment.

What I have found since that day is that I hold intentions a little more loosely and I form them with a lot more willingness to let them change as I go. For instance, rather than seeking clarity about a decision I am trying to

31

make so I can then go act on that, I will instead go about seeking clarity about the choices that I have before me and suspend the decision-making for another time. It leaves the wayfinding more open to the path and less about a destination.

When I choose an intention, I often just pick a word I like. For my longer DIY Pilgrimage, I chose the word "home." It carried all sorts of meanings for me as I walked from my home to my sister's, along many paths so familiar they felt like home. Sometimes, it's an attitude I wish to practice, like "openness." Other times, it's something I want more of in my personal or professional life, like "calm."

Before you walk today, decide on an intention. If you are not well-practiced at choosing an intention, set "awareness" as your intention. Walk to become more aware of what is going on around you and within you. Walk to become more aware of your surroundings. Walk to become more aware of what you experience in your body. Or use your own intention for this walk.

[walk here]

What is your intention for your walk today?

How will you hold your intention as you walk?

How did your intention change or stay the same as you walked today?

Lea looking over a road overpass on a long walk.

CHAPTER 7
PAY ATTENTION

Paying attention is a form of reciprocity with the living world, receiving the gifts with open eyes and open heart.

—Robin Wall Kimmerer,
Braiding Sweetgrass

Attention takes practice. It is the art of focusing on what you notice. As you begin walking regularly with the intention of building awareness, it is often beneficial to start with what is outside of you. We can use our physical senses to pay attention.

When I walk in my neighborhood, I notice a new plant next to a driveway, the color of a freshly painted front door, old chalk drawings on the sidewalk still visible after the rain, detritus in the gutter, the passing of the seasons on the peach tree around the corner. Some of these things may not be noticed by everyone as they pass by, but for me they do spark creativity in my thought process. My sights in my neighborhood are always changing and that keeps my walks more interesting to me.

Take a walk around your neighborhood and imagine it as a feast for your senses. Take in all that is around you. Notice sights and smells. Notice color and texture. Notice what you hear—is it nature, people, machines? Can you smell the scent of cooking or flowers blooming or automobile exhaust?

One day I decided to photograph the colors saw and I created a Rainbow Walk. On the first day, I photographed things that were red. They were natural, like a flower, or human created, like a red door down the street. And each day I looked for (and found) all the colors of the rainbow: red, orange, yellow, green, blue, indigo, violet. It was fun and it gave me an external focus for my walks that week.

I invite you to create your own themed walk with whatever interests you so that you create the opportunity to pay attention. You are looking, listening, and paying attention for what you hope to find.

[walk here]

What did you see? What did you hear?
What did you smell?

Is there any pattern you can draw from all of
these?

What might the things that caught your
attention tell you about yourself?

CHAPTER 8
WHAT YOU NOTICE

What we do with our attention is at the heart of what it means to be human.

—Rob Walker, *The Art of Noticing*

In the previous chapter I invited you to pay attention to what you experience around you as you walk. The next step is the noticing of what's going on in your body. This is another type of attention, but focused inward rather than outward towards your surroundings.

Often when a person is learning to meditate, they are invited to focus on their breath or a particular part of their body. This is likely because focused attention, noticing that your body exists or that you often breathe without thinking, is the opening to awareness. As you pay attention to how you are breathing when you walk, notice what else is going on in your body.

My body is always talking to me, so to speak. My knees and hips complain when I walk. My stomach is usually hungry and telling me so. The first Wayfinding Day I walked this year had me experiencing fatigue in a way I hadn't previously. I noticed I was tired. I noticed I was in a hurry to get this long walk over with because I feared I was developing a blister. I slowed down and noticed that as my steps became more deliberate, I also became more thoughtful. So, you start with your physical, embodied experience, and then move inward to thoughts and feelings.

[walk here]

What physical sensations do you experience in your body?

Have a conversation with a part of your body. What is it telling you?

CHAPTER 9
CREATE AWARENESS

Let us not look back in anger, nor forward in fear, but around in awareness.

—James Thurber

Awareness takes cultivation. Even when I walk the same pathways in our local wilderness park, I see different things each time. And it's not that the landscape has changed all that drastically since the week before.

I notice different things in my body as well. Maybe my sleep was interrupted the night before, so I am tired. Perhaps a workout earlier in the week has aggravated my knee so I'm limping a little while I get warmed up.

I am also more aware of my thoughts and feelings. Each time I begin a Wayfinding Day by myself, I recognize both my privilege and my vulnerability. Some walk with more physical pain, some with less. Others walk with more comfort and safety, some with less. All this awareness that comes from setting intentions and paying attention and noticing what is going on within me, means that I am often a little uncomfortable as I begin. It takes a little while to subside before I can settle into my walking.

The difficulty of settling in can often be found in what is on your mind or in your heart from before you started walking. It may be a recent problem at work or a conversation with a loved one that weighs on you. I am often surprised when the things that I carry in my heart come to the surface when I start to walk. As the minutes and miles go by, I find that I can let that go.

It's usually the combination of noticing things I see and hear along my walk, along with what I notice I am experiencing in my body, that gets me somewhere deeper. This moves me from one type of awareness to another. Sometimes my awareness is pleasant; sometimes I don't like what I notice in myself. I have learned to accept my discomfort if that is where I am and wait as I walk for it to subside. The longer I walk, the more likely it will.

Try it and see.

[walk here]

What is something that you need to complete that has been left undone that will allow you to be more present?

What are you thinking as you walk?

What are you feeling as you walk?

What else do you notice?

Lea's shadow on the San
Clemente, CA, boardwalk.

CHAPTER 10
ACCEPTANCE

The first step towards change is awareness. The second step is acceptance.

—Nathaniel Branden

What's quite interesting to me about walking regularly and often for a long stretch during a day, is that it I've genuinely come to like it.

I mentioned previously that I arrived at walking reluctantly because of the limits of my body and then found a rhythm when preparing for my Camino experience. But I continue to avidly walk because of all the benefits that I've experienced, primarily the awareness and connection I get with myself and the world around me. As I reflect on walking for this book, I also realize that part of the joy of walking for me is that I have accepted my body's limitations.

There's no more dreaming of marathons for me, and yet I can confidently plan to try for the Camino again in the coming years, pandemic and other global concerns allowing. While these limitations sometimes makes me sad, I find I have much more gratitude for what I can do, than regret for what I cannot do.

In some ways, walking has ushered in a whole new realm of physical experiences and opportunities for me that I really had not considered before. It also provides the chance to really listen to my body (and my mind, since I haven't quite gotten over the years of separating them into two!).

I've come to accept when my intentions dissolve or my experience goes sideways— like my first Wayfinding Day of 2024, that really was not all that fun. But I look back on that particular day with fondness for the fact that I got to do it, for what I saw and what I thought about, for what I learned about myself. Really, for simply being able to walk.

When you walk, you may not know what you are wanting or needing to accept. It may show up in unexpected ways, like it did for me the first time. I went walking and wayfinding to help calm my mind and get some answers to questions that seemed to jostle around inside my head. And I found some peace—and that was partly due, I realize now, to my acceptance of my situation.

Maybe that's part of walking slowly, and not being able to get anywhere in a hurry. Walking is not particularly efficient by 21st-century standards. We already must accept that we will get somewhere at a pretty slow pace. And Wayfinding Days are really walking experiences to simply help you be present in this point in time, not looking forward, not looking back.

[walk here]

What does your walk help you come to terms with?

How can you accept that you are just in this moment and not in the past or in the future?

How does walking help you accept your body and your mind and your thoughts and feelings?

CHAPTER 11
BE PRESENT

Pres ·ent par ·ti ·ci ·ple

noun

GRAMMAR

*1. the form of a verb, ending in -ing in
English, which is used in forming
continuous tenses, e.g. in I'm thinking.*

Walking is a continuous tense, and at least while we are actually walking, it often feels not bound by time.

In many ways our lives are also continuous tenses—always growing and changing, never stopping until we finally stop breathing and functioning as a human being. Maybe that's why I find walking such a profound experience. Walking at a pace that nearly matches my heartbeat, I find that I am in sync with myself, as if walking were just another extension of breathing, and breathing the continuous tense of living.

Walking is very much an act of being present. It is an opportunity to take the brain part of our body and bring it with us as we walk. My brain is very good at getting ahead of myself into the future or lagging behind, dwelling in the past. When I walk, perhaps because the pace is slower than a lot of our regular life activities, I know that my mind is usually able to keep up or slow down, whatever is needed that day.

I think it is no coincidence that the example the dictionary provides is the word, "thinking." Of all the -ing words in the English language, "thinking" was chosen. I wonder how many of us do that on continuous loop? I'm not saying we shouldn't think, but there are other ways of knowing, and walking may give us access to some of them.

When you walk, do so in the moment. When thoughts arrive, notice them and invite them to move aside. Notice your breathing, feel your heartbeat, check your pulse. Be in your body, your mind, your heart, your spirit, as you are living in the continuous tense of the moment.

[walk here]

Write a thank-you note to yourself for showing up to walk today.

CHAPTER 12
HOW TO PRACTICE

Practice, practice, practice!

—Every music teacher & sports coach
everywhere

We use the term practice in a number of different ways. I call my business my coaching practice. I talk about walking as a mindful practice. As people, we can practice gratitude, patience, or compassion. We can practice our skills in basketball or a musical instrument.

When you think about your own walking, establishing some sort of routine or practice is an end in itself. It is also great preparation for a longer Wayfinding Day.[1] From my own experience, walking regularly makes the longer Wayfinding Days better—you've exercised your body and your mind, and you've practiced paying attention and noticing so the experience is deeper and richer for it.

Now that you've explored intention and attention, noticing and awareness, and hopefully you've been able to experience the presence of walking, you can decide if you like it enough to do it regularly.

---

[1] It's always a good idea to consult a medical provider to be sure you are ready for any new levels of physical exercise you decide to undertake.

Do you want to create a regular walking routine? Do you want to prepare for a longer Wayfinding Day? If so, the following are some notes on how to establish the rhythm of practice, the doing of something again and again, paying attention and noticing each time your own experience of walking.

As a former music teacher, I know something about practice. First, most of us don't like to do it. Practice feels boring. It can be frustrating. It's the same stuff over and over and the improvement is there one day and not the next. But practice works over time. If you only look at a snapshot of practice, it will only show you where you are for that one day. If you look at your arc of practice over time, you will see where you've been and where you can go.

When I was teaching flute at the local community music school, I had lots of ideas for how to get kids (and grown-ups) to practice.

1. Attach your practice time to something you are already doing, such as before or after a meal.
2. Try for more often and less long—consistency is key.
3. It's ok if you aren't perfect at getting this going—keep at it!
4. If you miss a day, or a week, just start over.

You can use these practice tips if you are trying to start a regular walking routine. The more consistent you are at putting on your walking shoes and heading out the door, the easier it will be to do so even if the weather isn't great, or your feet hurt, or you feel rushed to complete another task after you get back.

There's something to be said about Nike's slogan, "Just Do It!" but you've got to do it again and again to make it a practice. Think about ways you can make walking fun or interesting or more compelling. Some people really go towards the fitness end of things in order to keep at walking. While that may certainly be a benefit you might experience, I encourage you to think about walking as a mindful practice, instead.

[walk here]

Here are some questions you can ask yourself regularly each time you walk (you'll notice some repetition from previous chapters here):

What do you see?

What do you hear?

What do you smell?

What do you notice inside you?

What are you thinking?

What are you feeling?

What do you experience in your body?

What else do you notice?

What questions arise as you walk?

CHAPTER 13

HAVE WONDER

Always be on the lookout for the presence of wonder.

—E. B. White

Walking is relatively accessible. It also is pretty inexpensive. You usually don't have to pay to have access to public spaces to walk. Most cities have public parks and many of us are close to some sort of larger spaces than our neighborhood provides. But neighborhoods are great! And walking where you live is an ideal way to develop connection to place, green space or not. When you travel slowly through the spaces where you live, you can pay attention more closely and notice what you might not see otherwise. Walking can be a way to become familiar.

A few years ago, prior to my DIY Pilgrimage, I was walking daily in my neighborhood. I'd loop as many different ways as I could through the streets of my suburban area. I'm also close to a city park, so would often end up there for a few loops around the dirt path (5x=1 mile!) where I'd see pine and citrus and snowy mountains or blue sky through the trees. I could feel far away on these walks.

After you've taken your inventory of what you can take in, find a place to sit and ponder. Ponder means to think carefully or to weigh a decision. It is the heavy lifting of thought. It is the "figure it out" approach. After you ponder, I invite you to wonder.

Wonder is linked to curiosity and intellectual exploration. It moves towards imagination and discovery—so you can find out rather than figure out. This is what happens for me on wayfinding days because I am a very "figure it out" kind of person. I ponder and think and try, try, try to make sense of it all. And when I walk, I am able to let go and begin to wonder with more ease. Wonder as you walk.

Let's play with this a little. There are six letters of the alphabet in between P and W. Write an acrostic poem where each line begins with the letter from P through W, to help you get from Ponder to Wonder.

Here's one I wrote for you:

Ponder what is going on in you

Query your thoughts

Restore your confidence in yourself

Sit with it and simmer

Trust yourself

Uncover what's really there

Verdant soil of possibility

Wonder at it all

Now it's your turn:

P

Q

R

S

T

U

V

W

CHAPTER 14
GROW YOUR CURIOSITY

Truth walks toward us on the paths of our questions.

—Jacqueline Winspear

In a recent conversation with a coach friend of mine, we talked about curiosity as one of the motivators to help people try new things.

While we noted a number of things that can help someone get started, curiosity was one of the primary ones. Curiosity is the openness to ask questions of yourself, your surroundings, and your world. From these questions you can gain awareness and insight. When you walk, seek the questions more than the answers.

For some of you, curiosity may be what is fueling your interest in walking as you ask, with what, after all, do you occupy yourself for hours at a time while walking for most of the day? My answer is that you occupy yourself! Your mind, your desires, your wonderings, all become inhabitable when given the time to explore. And curiosity takes us there.

This book has provided some prompts for questions before, during and after you walk. You are welcome to ask these same questions over and over. In fact, some of them lend themselves to repetition each time you walk, like the following:

What is your intention for this walk?
What way are you looking to find?
Or the questions that check in with your senses or the parts of yourself from Chapter 12, "How to Practice."

But what if you want more? Make them up based on what you experience while you walk. Wayfinding in the traditional sense is looking for signs to help you find your direction to something you are looking for. One way I practice wayfinding when I walk is to see the signs and ask the questions that come from my curiosity.

This makes wayfinding fun for me. I have the intention to notice signs and therefore I am more aware of my surroundings. I have the intention to notice what goes on inside of me once I see those signs, and thus I am more aware of myself. I am much more prone to make meaning out of something I see rather than believe that I noticed it for a reason. The meaning that I make from these signs while I walk is in direct correlation to how focused my attention and intention are.

Here's an example of an internal conversation I had on a recent Wayfinding Day as a demonstration of how you could do this, too.

"That sign is cool." It reads,
BEGIN.

"I wonder what I need/want to begin right now in my life?"
I keep walking.

The next sign I notice is END.
"Hmmmm. When do I end the actions I'm thinking about?"

Which leads me to ask, "How do I know when to start something and when to end something? So many things to consider...."

The next sign I see is STOP. "Ah! I want to stop trying to figure this out." I keep walking.

Then I see a sign with an arrow pointing to the right towards a city park. I turn and head that way leaving my ponderings at the base of that STOP sign. On to the next Wayfinding moment.

At the park I see a group of adults playing a pick-up soccer game. I began to wonder about the ways

humans like to have fun as I
enjoy seeing the enjoyment
they are having together.

One way to use the signs you notice is to have them invite the questions. And then connect the questions as you find your way (both externally and internally) while you walk.

Another way to be curious is to prep your questions ahead of time. What has been on your mind recently? What questions in life won't let you go? Is there a decision that you are trying to make? I've had less success at getting anywhere with these kinds of questions because I get happily distracted with what I notice around me and that takes me back to the kind of internal conversation like I shared above. Preparing my questions ahead of time does work sometimes for me, especially on shorter walks, however.

[walk here]

What kinds of questions do you ask yourself
as you walk?

What does the meaning you give the signs
that you see suggest to you?

How might these signs help you find your way?

Participants in a small group Wayfinding Day resting and writing in their journals at Crystal Cove State Park, CA.

CHAPTER 15
READ THE SIGNS

Words are but the signs of ideas.

—Samuel Johnson

You can connect the signs you see along your walk as you go or after you get back for a different type of wayfinding. I call it wayfinding after the fact! Here is an example of how I have done this previously and how you could try it next time you walk.

On my very first Wayfinding Day, the intent was to walk and to stop every hour to journal what I was noticing internally. The first few hours were bustling with noise and commotion since it was a beautiful February weekend day after lots of rain. People were out and about and enjoying the sunshine. I found it difficult to notice what was going on inside of me. I wrote about what I saw around me instead.

What's funny to me now is one of my journal entries was simply signs I saw along the way:

- We Serve Brunch on Weekends

- Save the Bay Aquarium

- Cleanse your Chakras

• Come Pray with Us

• Wish You Were Here

In trying to connect my thoughts on these signs—serve + save + cleanse + pray + wish—I think I discovered what my Wayfinding Day provided for me. After I recorded those signs in my journal, I walked in silence and in peace. I went walking that day to find something in the immensity of the ocean and the expansiveness of the sand. Instead, I found the quiet within my own self.

On one of my small group Wayfinding Days there were signs that indicated that a section of beach was a "Clarifier." Even though I had walked that way before, I don't remember noticing those signs previously. I immediately began to wonder to myself how walking on this beach, with the sand and water, could be a clarifying experience for me.

Sign reading "Clarifier" at Huntington Beach, CA.

I see signs reminding me to slow down, to stop, to yield, to merge, to mind my speed, to protect an endangered species, as well as signs for restrooms and restaurants. Ah, rest comes next! But before that…

[walk here]

Ocean clarity measures the amounts of particles (like plankton, bacteria they call "suspended particles") that are floating in the water. What are the suspended particles that get in the way of your clarity?

What signs do you notice today as you walk? Write them down or take photos of them. When you get back, reflect on the kinds of meaning you see in them for yourself now.

CHAPTER 16
TAKE A REST

The most valuable thing we can do for the psyche, occasionally, is to let it rest, wander, live in the changing light of room, not try to be or do anything whatever.

—May Sarton

An important thing about my Wayfinding Days is to have moments of rest. Taking breaks is important. I eat (snacks and meals), and walk and wonder, write and reflect, talk with people I am walking with or I meet along the way. Or just sit and take in the beauty around me. Stopping is a part of walking, really. We are not machines and cannot just walk all day long without rest. It's like that in life, as well. Sometimes we walk to rest our minds and sometimes we rest to let our minds wander.

A lot of my coaching clients talk about needing to pause, to collect their thoughts, to connect with what they are feeling, to calm their nerves. They pause in presentations, in conversations, in meetings. This pause is empowering. It helps them get back their nerve or their confidence. It helps them communicate better. It helps them notice what is going on inside and around them.

Taking rests in life is important, too. Sleep is one of the main issues that is shared by many of the clients I work with. They don't sleep well, usually because of worry. Sometimes they have medical issues or other physical problems like extensive pain that are problematic. But working on sleep hygiene is one way to gain back some measure of control of our lives. I can pretty much guarantee that after walking for an entire Wayfinding Day, most everyone sleeps well. We're not exhausted like a backpacker might feel in the High Sierra, or fully spent like a marathoner, but rather just tired, needing that pause called a good night's sleep.

Which leads me back to the ways we walk. Whether we amble or stroll, shuffle or skip our way through life, we ought to be tired at the end of the day. That's how it should be,

I think. We exert energy, we are soothed, we get invigorated, and we rest. It is a cycle—physical, mental, spiritual. Noticing the cycle is like meditation. Breathing in, breathing out. One foot in front of the other.

Receiving, giving back. Connecting within ourselves and to the whole world. Finding clarity and calm. As Thich Nhat Hanh, a Buddhist monk who wrote often of walking, writes, we say "yes" as we breathe in and "thank you" as we breathe out. Receiving the goodness of the day's walk and then responding with gratitude.

[rest here]

What do you say 'yes' to today?

What are you thankful for?

Sign reminding us to, "Stop your engine. Set your brake." While resting on the Balboa Island Ferry, Newport Beach, CA.

CHAPTER 17
INSIGHT GAINED

Insight perceives…wisdom knows.

—Matshona Dhliwayo

If you've read this book in chapter order, you've walked over a dozen times now. What do you think? Want to keep going?

If you decided to respond to the questions I posed in each chapter, you've also done quite a bit of reflection. If you came up with your own questions, you've reflected even more.

Where does this leave us? Wayfinding is so much more than a destination, so the purpose of this book isn't necessarily to get you somewhere, but rather to get you going, help you get started. And maybe walking and wayfinding will be something that you'll like, because don't we all know that when we enjoy something we're more apt to do it! And even if you don't love it, perhaps there has been something that has piqued your interest or compelled you in one way or another.

Wayfinding is more than a frolic in the park (ooh, I'll have to add that one to my walking word list). Wayfinding takes some work. It gets us out of our heads and the thinking traps and the circular reasoning that causes us to feel stuck and invites us into a deeper knowing of ourselves. As we pay attention, notice, and become more aware, we begin to find our way. Maybe it is another move from P to W—we move from perception to wisdom when we walk again and again and again.

As our perception deepens, our wisdom grows, and we discover ways of knowing beyond that "figuring it out" mode that I started with at the beginning of my wayfinding journey. In addition, we often gain insight into our relation to the world around us.

I've written often throughout this book about my connection to place, but I don't have a chapter on location. I've done that (mostly) deliberately because there are so many places throughout the world and so many places with which each of us feels connection. I didn't think I could address them all, so I leave you with some thoughts, instead.

Connection to place happens when we spend time somewhere. It occurs when we pay attention to things as we walk because we are going more slowly. Connection to place happens as we get more connected to ourselves, at least that is what has occurred for me with wayfinding. I can't help but think it is in some ways attending to the very desire that I had when I set out on my first DIY Pilgrimage—I wanted to find home: in myself, in my body, on the paths and roads I was walking upon, in the relationships with the people I love.

As we end this conversation, as books are after all dialogs between authors and readers, I wish you many long days of walking, much awareness of who you are and who you wish to become, and a connection to the ground upon which you move!

[walk here]

Ask your own questions now.

CHAPTER 18
DIY WAYFINDING DAY TIPS

*Between every two pines
is a doorway to a new world.*

—John Muir

The openings that we seek when we go on a walk can be found in nature between the trees. But I believe the doorways to deeper knowing and reflective listening to our hearts is also found through garden gates, and over bridges, and along sidewalks and the sides of roads. You can create a Wayfinding Day anywhere.

When you do this on your own, there is a separate step of preparation. And in order for you to be able to take it all in, you've got to do the prep work. Check the maps multiple times, plan a route with back-up plans, prepare for something to not quite go as planned, so that when you are in it, you can receive the gift of the time you have allowed for yourself.

To create the best wayfinding day for yourself is to set aside more time than you need so that you won't be squished from the edges of the day. If you've got something going on in the evening, it may not be the best day for wayfinding. But, if that's all you can do on that particular day and you don't have the option, then just plan for something shorter so you leave enough buffer to have space for transformation.

It's hard to have calm when you are in a hurry. Walk slowly. Plan to walk slowly. Allow for rest. Plan to stop to reflect, to think, to hydrate and eat, to sit in silence. Many adults can walk three miles in one hour. But take your time. Give yourself time. Plan for more time than you think you could possibly need to walk three miles! It isn't a fitness routine where you are trying to get your heart rate up. You are actually trying to get it to slow, to get your mind to slow down and your body to just be in the moment.

Let me repeat. Don't be in a hurry. If you only have an hour, then choose to walk only one mile, rather than trying to squeeze in a workout. Wayfinding Days are not workouts. They are reflective, contemplative, mindful walking experiences. They are opportunities to move your body, to move your heart, to quiet your mind.

And expect surprises. On my very first Wayfinding Day I was certain that I would find clarity on an answer I was seeking. That was the point of my walking that day. I intended to think and write and reflect and repeat that process over and over. And instead, I just needed time to be with myself. To stop the reflection cycle in the middle and just be with the thoughts and see where they took me. And then to let them go. Ultimately, I needed time to just be. I found peace of mind. And that was the clarity that I needed. I found calm. And the clarity that came to me was that I needed calm. I needed peace. I didn't need more ideas, or reflections, or thoughts, or action plans (sorry, Coach Lea!).

What's wonderful about Wayfinding Days, however, is that you can find what you need even if it is different than what I needed. Movement allows our bodies to unwind a little. It shakes out the crooks in our necks and lets our thoughts settle. When you walk, you will know. And if the answer is another question, then that's exactly what you needed. And if the answer is quiet, then that's what you needed. Often our body knows what we need. We just have to give it a bit of space and time to become aware. And insight will come.

Here is a list of some things to think about as you plan out a longer walking experience:

1) Pick a day with fewer responsibilities.

2) Adjust your time/length of your walk based on your responsibilities, your fitness, and personal desires for the experience.

3) Choose a new day, if necessary.

4) Plan a route that you enjoy—it honestly doesn't really matter where it is.

5) Choose a route where you have access to restrooms, water, and people (for safety's sake, unless you are a well-experienced hiker and have appropriate GPS tools in case of emergency, and know how to use them).

6) Spend some time looking online or at paper maps to decide on the best route.

7) Make a back-up plan.

8) Make a safety plan (let someone know where you are going, an itinerary, and a timeline).

9) Adjust your day or schedule based on weather forecast.

10) Leave your headphones at home, but bring a device for maps, weather, photos, and emergencies.

11) Bring a backpack or hip pack to carry appropriate gear: sunscreen, hat, snacks, water, this book (!), journal, etc.

12) When you start, take a breath and then let your planning go…it's time to implement.

13) Make regular stops to read through your questions or to consider what you've noticed and what questions come to mind.

14) Be sure to rest and eat and hydrate.

15) At the end of your wayfinding day, take note of the way that you found. Be grateful. Celebrate.

Waiting for the train in Solana
Beach, CA, after a DIY Pilgrimage.

AFTERWORD

What does it mean to be connected to place?

A number of people who read my book wanted to put an "a" in front of the word "place." But there is a giant difference to me in being connected to a place or even a bunch of places and being connected to place (which is for me kind of a plural term).

Being connected to place is wide and deep–it's a multi-dimensional connection that is more than physical or emotional. I think it definitely is spiritual, as well.

So why don't you just say connected to places?

Well, that means separate individual places and that's not quite what I mean either. It is a collective, really. Both individual places and all the places as a whole. So, saying I am connected to place is kind of a grounding statement for me. It's probably a lot more philosophical and goes beyond memories or good experiences or even a longing to be in a particular place. It's kind of like that place is always in me and maybe a part of me is in all those places that I feel connection with.

Other people who use the term connected to place often are talking about responsibility for the land, or a cultural connection over time. I think it is that for me, too.

Connection to place animates the locations, by which I mean it brings them to a life of their own not just in relation to me.

So how do other people become connected to place through walking?

I think it is the slow, deliberate, getting to know a place in relation to self. Being connected to place has something to do with love, I think. So, by walking a person can lovingly, carefully, slowly, know all the nooks and crannies along the side of a road and follow the contours of path.

Maybe when I say I am connected to place, I am saying that I am home...in myself and in the space around me. May you find your way home.

ACKNOWLEDGMENTS

A book doesn't come to fruition all by itself. It's been a collective walking experience. Thank you to my regular walking partner, Rebecca, since a book about walking is decidedly better when grounded in the actual experience of putting shoe to pavement or boot to trail.

To my first Wayfinding Day participants— thank you for trusting me to take you on a walk together and for your feedback that has found its way into this book. And to my coaching clients who do lots of indoor wayfinding that always inspires and refreshes my thinking.

Thanks to my REI friends and colleagues who remind me that walking, along with most outdoor adventures, is a complicated business connected to our social fabric—the unraveled, the torn, and the mended.

To my Erickson International coach colleagues—Christine, Dana, Lana, Lily, Martina, Nadja, Sarah, Yulia—you've been witness to the unfolding of this journey. Thank you for asking all the right questions to help me query further and deeper into what I really want.

And thank you to my family: Billy, my partner in all sorts of adventures; my kids—Samantha, Elliott, and Owen—who have put up with Mom's wild ideas for getting out and about over the years; my parents, Ann and Rick, for believing in me from day one; and my sister Sara, who helped me understand the badassery of women who walk.

Special thanks to Sharon Graff for her wisdom and support over the years and to my artist niece Carolyn Knapp, for the cover design.

ABOUT THE AUTHOR

 **Lea Appleton** is a 4th-generation Southern Californian connected to place through walking— from the beaches of the Pacific Ocean to the pinnacles of the High Sierra mountain range. She spent a couple of decades in theological higher education, helping to build multicultural and interreligious communities, and now is a professional certified coach in private practice helping working professionals live meaningful lives. She also works in the outdoor industry. Lea has a Master of Arts in Music, a Master of Divinity degree, and holds the Professional Certified Coach (PCC) credential from the International Coaching Federation. Lea lives with her husband Billy and has three adult children.

For more information about coaching for a better day at work or for how to participate in a guided Wayfinding Day, visit Lea's website at www.appletoncoaching.com or connect on socials:

Instagram: @appletoncoaching

Facebook: @appletoncoaching

LinkedIn: @lea-appleton

Made in the USA
Columbia, SC
26 May 2024

36204214R00083